Tai

Written by Jo Windsor

Here is a crocodile.
Look at the tail!

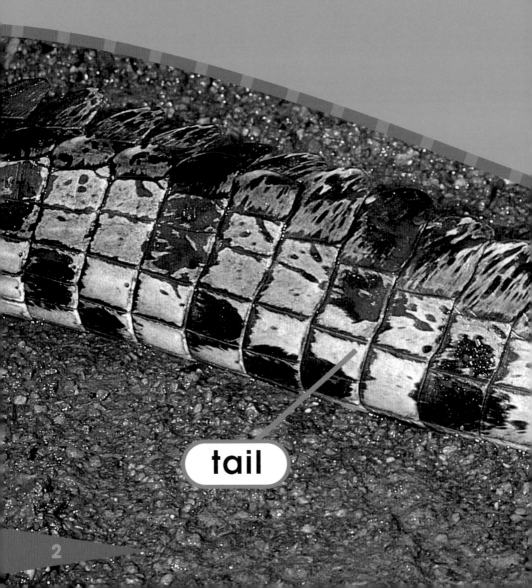

tail

Here is a giraffe.
Look at the tail!

tail

4

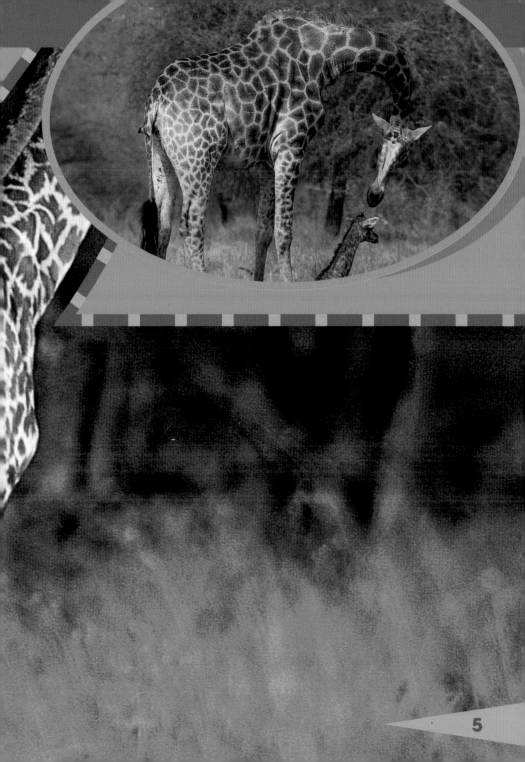

Here is a monkey.
Look at the tail!

tail

Here is a zebra.
Look at the tail!

tail

Here is a fox.
Look at the tail!

tail

Here is a whale.
Look at the **big** tail!

tail

Index

▬▬ Guide Notes

Title: Tails

Stage: Emergent – Magenta

Genre: Nonfiction (Expository)

Approach: Guided Reading

Processes: Thinking Critically, Exploring Language, Processing Information

Written and Visual Focus: Photographs (static images), Index, Labels

Word Count: 49

FORMING THE FOUNDATION

Tell the children that this book is about animals' tails.

Talk to them about what is on the front cover. Read the title and the author.

Focus the children's attention on the index and talk about the animals that are in this book.

"Walk" through the book, focusing on the photographs and talk about the different tails the animals have.

Read the text together.

THINKING CRITICALLY

(sample questions)

After the reading

• Why do you think an animal might need a tail?

• Which animal do you think might use its tail the most and why?

EXPLORING LANGUAGE

(ideas for selection)

Terminology

Title, cover, author, photographs

Vocabulary

Interest words: crocodile, tail, giraffe, monkey, zebra, fox, whale

High-frequency words: here, is, a, look, at, the